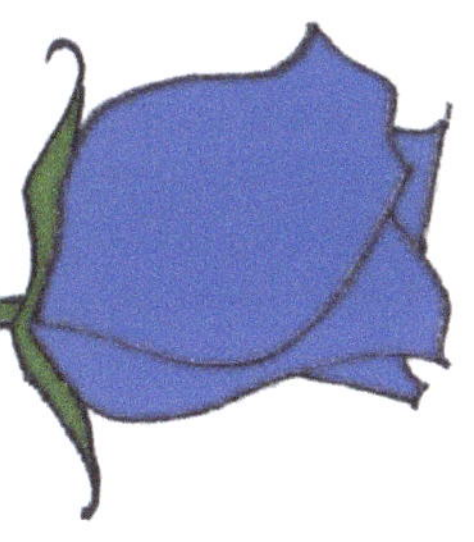

Blue Roses

Y. Zambrano

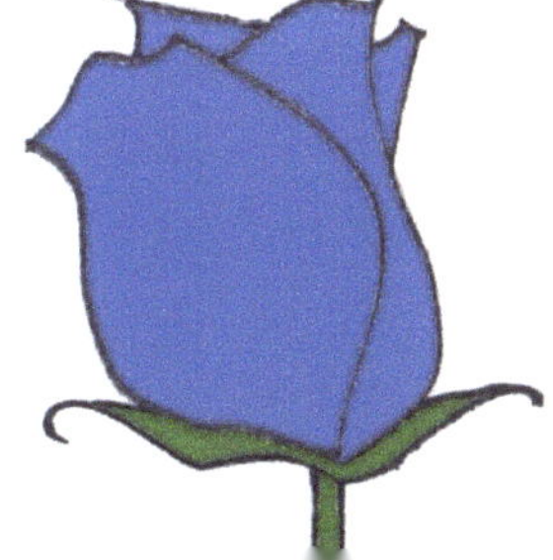

Editor: **Ashley Jane/Ashley Jane Aesthetics**

Blue Roses
Y. Zambrano
1st Edition

ISBN: 978-0-578-75052-1

She is healing.

She is grounding.

She graces every part of me.

She is love.

She is Serenity.

She sings in shades of the sky.

She takes control.

She is my breath and makes me new.

She is the Ocean.

She is Blue.

Freedom
is the words you write with in ink.

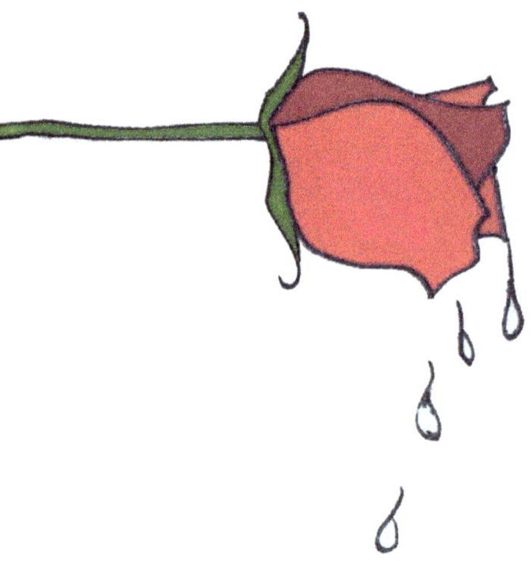

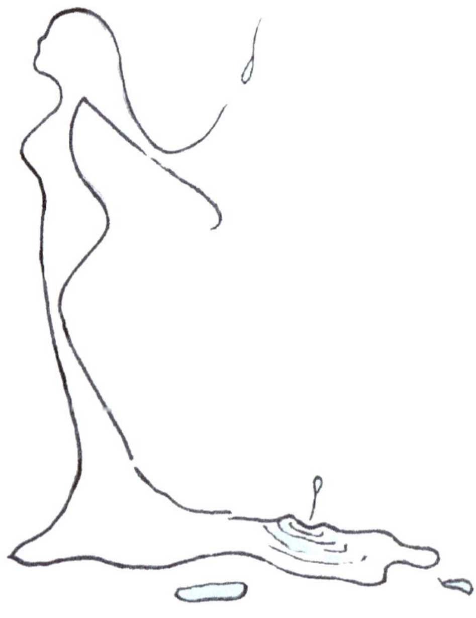

Rain drops of red
and she
becomes the rose of roses.

Whiskey

Whiskey
of
ballet at the waterway.
Smoothly it goes.
Silence the days.
Whiskey written as cigarette amour.
Hold me tight.
A poet who kisses the night.
Every word poured.
It's the only diary known.
Cherry at the bottom
and
Whiskey
of
nights with me.

Before Nights Begin

Dusk falls with silence along the Sun.
How much truth does it speak?
Lips taste of perfume.
A belly full of dark keeps.
The sabotage is golden,
and I have spilled my ink.

Wake

Wake me up
from this dream that haunts this heart.
Wake me up
from this nightmare that keeps my soul apart.

Awaken I then become,
but the racing of my heart
spears into these scars.
My stomach flutters with agony.
My visions get the best of me.
These dreams and this reality have formed
some sort of bond.

Wake me up
from these dark gray rooms that tap against
these tender arms.
Wake me up
from the empty drops that remind me,
I am seating for one.

Awaken I then become.
As I gaze beside me,
the conversation becomes none

Silence fills all along these walls.

The cold space has invited herself to run along.
I scream inside to be left alone.

Wake me up,
wake me up.

Oh,
please wake me up.

Awaken I then become.

Black Rose

The clinch against my skin.
Red tears running down my fingertips.
Punctured on the inside.

Oh,
how your thorns are deep in.
Nighttime falls with the venom of your bud.
Sweet demons come purify my love.
Nothing ever felt so precise until I stumbled
upon your dark knight.

Intoxicating it is,

oh,

sweet black rose.

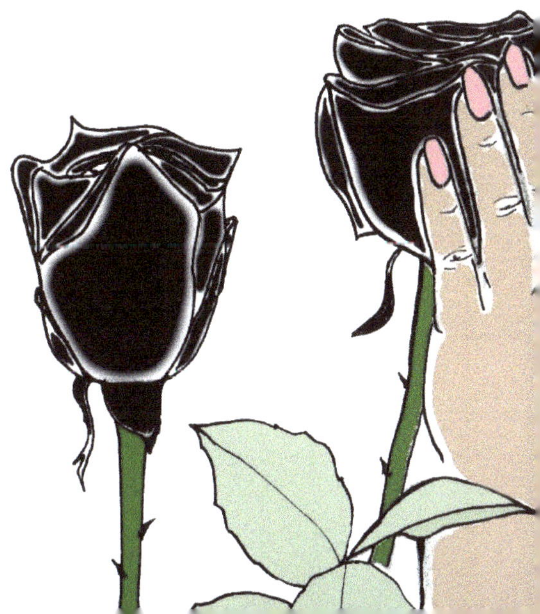

Midnight Black

Lick up the drops from my drips.
A midnight look made of stars.
Smell the midnight black in him,
a real gangster who writes his words
that pour like milk onto me.
Making me feel my own kind
of
beauty.

Secrets

Spanish secrets hidden away
as she starts dancing in the deep
and
they beg for mercy.

Brush of Fire

She!
A hurricane.
She sets flames.
She is her own woman.

She is the brush of fire.

Moon's Moth

In a night
from a blustering flame,
the moth fell in love with the moon
and began to seek its reply.

Thank You

And
in a way,
I have to thank you
for sending me on my way.

Thank you
for what you did,
for destroying every part of me.

So
thank you,
it's the very thing that set me free.

Darlene

Darlene,
the Darkling angel
whom brings us together
where only her wild roses grow.
Here in the damned,
she craves desires of dreams
from every one of those thorns.

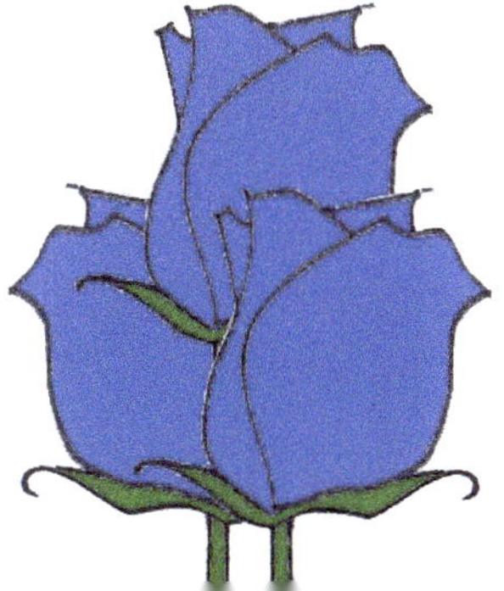

Dark Love

A dark past from a love,
one love.
Kissed by a ghost as I awoke.
Nothing followed,
just the cold air that kept in the volumes.
Rosy cheeks in a gray room.
How can I hide this?
These stains of written locks!
I taste it.
I feel it,
the way that it danced,
the way that it made my body crash.
With it,
without it.
Just one of one.

Goodbyes

The bridges we crossed
of ode goodbyes.
But something about this one felt different.
There's nothing more on my sleeve to say.
Let this be our last farewell.
It's almost done.
No tears as we turn away.
Reveries of yesterday.
Now and endlessly.

Friday's Love 13

Confidential magic,
a breath of poetry speaks the beauty of blue.
Ring of my soul.
Walking down a spiral of stairs in a white gown.
My feet touch the cold steps hinting at the
shades of it.
Moonlit waters talking low.
I miss you.
Gypsy love on whiskey nights.
Where are we to go?
Lick my fingers as I place them onto your lips,
tasting the way of my softness.
Set the haunting of its manner.
Unchaining the depth of breaths.
Inscriptions in a dim hallway
left with a trace of your grace.

Wait

Wait! But wait.
Do you really mean what you say?

Wait! Just wait.
Stop saying all those things.
What you say makes it hurt.

Wait! Please wait.
And think before you say those things.
The things that hurt.
Before it makes me go,
because I don't really want to go.

Wait! Just wait.

Rain Drops

I sit underneath this evening
with rain on my hands
and thick eyelids.
My head I lift and taste the drops
from a hurricane.
Winds carry its perfume
from a shadow of the storm.

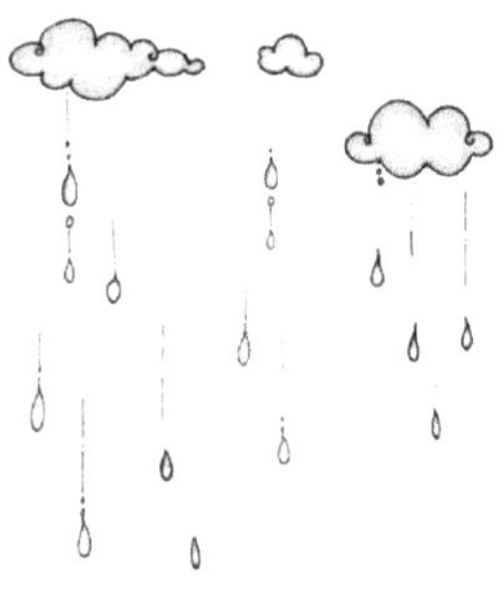

Paralyzed Soul

Acid drops onto the petals of my heart.
Oh,
forget me not!
Siren sounds through my eyes.
I licked the blood that was left on my lips.
Our love was reckless!
A steel door behind which I locked it away.
Just let the words burn slow.
The tears!
They lost this time,
and all I saw was my spirit leave.
Concrete and cigarette smoke, I wait in.
And
underneath it all,
my soul was paralyzed.

Rewind

She sings with whiskey breath
of dripping secrets.
Wild sunrise and summer wind,
she rides.
Fingertips run like sugar alongside.
Drift with it.
Desert feet.
A collection of her poetry.

Burning Love

It was the wolf in her
others couldn't resist.
Messy from the root,
but
only one burning desire.
One burning love
she feeds from.

Liquid Rubies

Rubies spilled from the corners of my mouth
leaving trails.
Liquid licks of cocaine sips.
They came to me crawling
with blood on their knees.
Touch me while I touch me.
Kisses on my feet as if I'm a Saint.
Drop flowers before me.
Impurity is in the ruby taste.

Remembrance

He's on the subway.
Eyes wander,
but he sealed up the only thing she gave him.
His eyes closed,
he carries her secret.
It beats every time.
Her heart!
The one that he still holds.
He took every deep breath of her in
for remembrance.

Caked Fields

Close-by winds caked the fields
with a dust of blue.
Gypsy dreams ripple close,
but still away.
Sunlight and shadow hint with whispers.
Lightning strikes in the height reached here,
just like the stroke of forever
walking back to my bare bones.

The Way the Waters Move
(Letters to the Ocean)

Sweet waters,
I emptied myself into
and
washed under its sun.
Divinity hits against my hips,
for my womb belongs to her.
My lips are fed with honey.
And in the way the waters move,
I
exhaled and emerged.
A rebirth with yellow roses.
Ocean,
I drink from the blue that is you,
but the letters are written to Oshun.

Eight Hours

Ticking.
Silent seas.

Eight hours;
meet with me,
guide me.
Here it comes.
Tamed winds.

Eight hours;
here,
there only lasts.
Same feel.

Eight hours of this embrace.
We have come home.
Moving with what stands of eight hours.

Same As

In the form of you
were a thousand love notes
meant to be read
by which I began to unfold,
falling straight through,
because
after all,
I am cut from the same cloth as you.

Pride

Flesh is my flesh.
Skin that glows.
For I am a woman of pride,
of utterly great pride.
The heart that I carry is of pure gold.
The loyalty that I give
cannot be compared to those.

Pride is my strength.
Pride is my weakness.
Pride is the whole of what I cannot say.
Pride is the hurt I give to those.
Pride is beauty,
and beauty is the pain I chose.

The smiles I give light up what I control.
Inside, I crave for what I will not say.
For what I will not show
is not what I want you to know.
Hands so soft,
eyes so brown.
It's rare to find one of my kind.

Great woman of pride
for I stay so true,
true to you.

For I still give all I carry inside.

Unconditional woman of pride.
Unconditional woman of love.
Of great love and great touch.

Woman of pride.
We only cry inside.
I give all I give with a sincere side.
For I love with pride and for pride I love.

Love, love, love.
Can you see this side?
A side I carry,
with a warmth that's like a fairy.

Prideful woman.
Heartfelt woman.
We are one of the same kind.

Rose Gold

Petal by petal
with one to hold;
the last one fallen.
It rains of holy water,
but it tastes like whiskey rose gold.

Museum of my Heart

Collected pieces.
A mosaic of hell,
but there is beauty
in the pain my heart held.

Glass Bones

Shattered.
A thousand pieces left on the bathroom floor.
Mirrored bones,
smeared reflection,
broken vanity breaths.
Waiting without any words.
Fallen to the bottom of the bottle.
Standing in glass.
I tried to bury the skeletons,
but I could hear it now.

Delicate

Please!
You can't stay.
Don't even look my way,
at least not now.
I am at a fragility.
I can't be around you right now.
Not while it's dark here.
You can't save me.
I can't even save me.
Don't stick around,
because it's all too delicate.
I don't know who I'll be tomorrow,
and you're too good to be here right now.
I'm sorry,
but this place that I am at is so cold.
Don't stay here.
Please!
You have to go.

Rain Song

Stoned on your love,
high on these violent songs.
Rain showers dropped
as I rose
and placed a crown onto my head.
Black roses fall,
and a kiss of death,
you fed.
Resurrect me
from
the sips of your cocaine rain song.

Murder Ballad

Walking towards the ocean
with my blue jeans still on,
there was a trade in the winds.
blue rust skies,
fallen butterflies,
words that were chosen to lead me.
I was sober this time,
from a touch on my fingertips
now tied to every daisy.
Slow motion murder ballad
here to hold me,
and I was ready.

Dancing Demons

In a field
where roses aren't red,
but it's the reaping of all that sowed.
He!
Born with fear
and scared of the things it made him do.
The dancing fire lead him to
his baptism by demons
he could not emerge from.

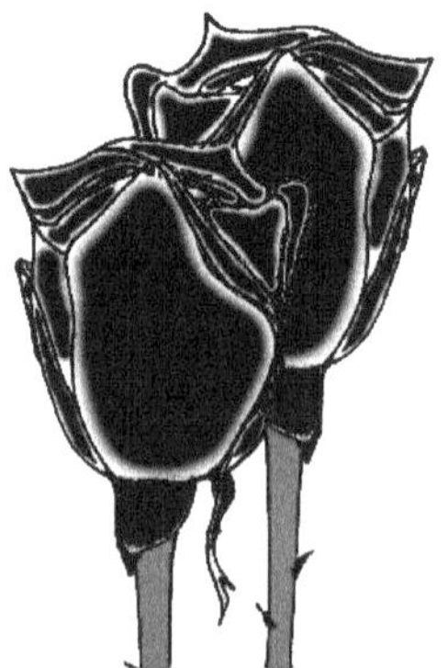

Reaching Out

It was a long walk,
and it rained that day.
A figure approached me
dressed in my favorite sins.
I tried reaching out to its sun in February,
but it was filled with black holes.
And I crowned the dark core of immoral
just once more.

Onto Me (You)

You.
Onto me like midnight seas in the way we collide.
You're beautifully damaged,
and it runs as strings of flowers all across me.
You feel like heaven with some sin.
By my heart I am here.
I give it all.

You.
Onto I hold as the darkest of hours gather.
Your words.
In the way that it feels,
write them for me.

You.
Find the way of myself.
Whispers.
They kiss while with
you.

Kissed

Shadow kissed,
promise slipped.
Love from a stairway of sins.
Separate your light.
Smoking on this last cigarette,
but
war lips tend to burn s l o w.

Blue Valentine

I've been driving,
driving to see my blue Valentine.
A song I have for him is on this woodnote
I carry tied with two red ribbons.
Each of these lines, he is in.
This song I write is only for him.

My blue Valentine,
such a gentle love,
such a true love,
such a look.
Complete, he and I are.
He is mine,
and I am his.

Only I understand the man behind
a blue Valentine.

Russian Roulette

I threw the deck
while they puffed on their cigars.
Soon it will be my turn.
Click, click,
only hollow points.
My palms are sweaty.
This may be my last one.
Here we go,
round and round.
Everyone's on the same ride.
Pain is the only language this room seeks.
Shot after shot.
Click!
The room goes dark.
Still only one in the chamber.

A Revolution

Right through the rain
which freed me from the pain.
Woke I am.
And after all those misplaced hours,
I found a voice,
marched against the crowd,
held up my own signs,
battled my way through.
A lioness born in the month of love.
I succeeded,
but first I had to let it kill me,
had to let it consume the depths of this soul.

But then again,
I
brought it back,
gave it life,
what was taken away
brick by brick,
uncovered those layers.

As I began,
I began again
and started waking up on my side of the bed
even more,
felt the comfort of my own covering.

The moon,
the stars,
they started to follow me furthermore.
I've seen the last page,
and of Judah,
HIS palm has been placed.

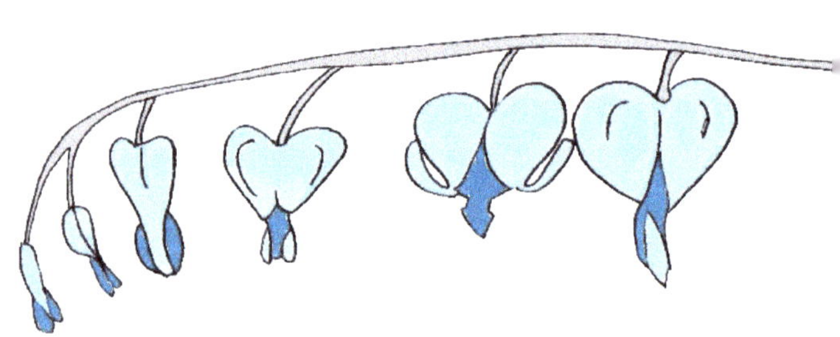

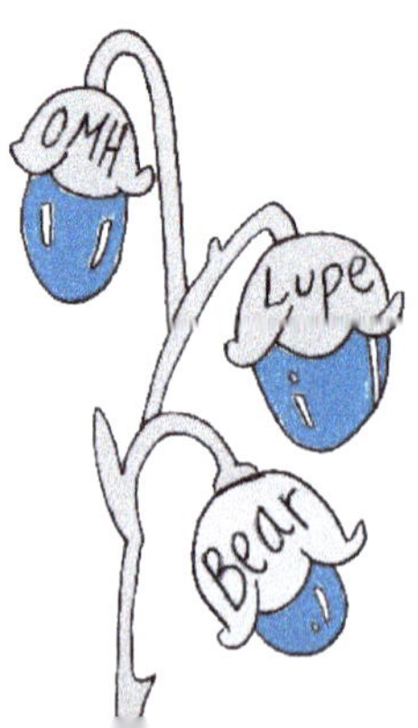
OMH
Lupe
Bear

Hallway

A midnight run.
One,
two,
and three.
My eyes meet here.
This hallway.
I have danced here before.
I walked with each:
you,
you,
and you as a child.
Here,
I feel it all.
Shadow souls of purity.
The colors on the walls look good here;
sweet canvas,
let it run.
Doors lead to laughter.
Rooms that carry from vein to vein.
This hallway of wildflowers.
Shadow souls are in my soul.

Closet

The lights are flickering.
I'm sitting in this closet
looking at this space.
Your side is empty.
I feel empty.
Not sure what it is that I did
to make you turn away from me?
Maybe I was too hard to love?
Maybe I was just too hard for you to love?
Empty hangers dangling in my face.
Empty shoe boxes I threw away.
You left your white tee behind.
I feel so little in this small space.
I seem to be frozen at this time.
Keys on the floor,
no knocks at the front door.
Staring into space with nothing to say.
I'm still sitting in this closet,
looking at this space.
It used to be our closet.
I still feel empty.

Silenced

Reasons rise with the moon.
Blank maps of silent streets waiting
with honeyed words
falling and fading.
The way it bleeds between the pages,
you can always smell the ink dry.
Come with me,
and feel the rush from
the falling of petals,
but listen to the silence
that comes from its poetry.
Take time in it,
and be gentle from it.
So acquainted.

Lightening Nights

The night is up,
even when we sleep.
Feeling it on my face,
breathing heavily in adoration.
The night crosses with lightning,
falling with its midnight rose
split down in two.
This night is the rubies
against my blood.
The night comes barefoot
running back to hear its screams.

Russian Doll

Blush red cheeks,
eyes bleeding in silence.
Layer after layer
calling to uncover every part of her layers.
Blessed with painted beauty
from poison and pearl.
A breath of the wild shimmers
that drip down her sides.
Piece by piece,
a vintage of each soul
reaching away into the days.

Moments of Madness

Here lies me - one, two, three.
Laughter shared with tears.
Can anyone hear
how the clown smears his name?
Sharp knives in room 29.
I now bleed in blue.
It wasn't at all how I pictured it to be.
Let me go!
I beg of you.
No response.
All I see are red lights.
Give me back life!
I might just do this line.
Not sure who I am anymore.
All I see are trapped doors
and checkered boards.
Follow it down this hallway.
Madness and insanity
pointed at my temple,
but I didn't tremble.

Ghost of Graves

The dress she wore is by the fireplace.
Her voice haunts the hallway.
Fevers at bedtime.
He weeps quietly
while sleeping next to her grave.
Lost eyes,
voices of MaryLou.
It rained of black roses,
and they danced at her tomb.

Cigarette

The smoke of this cigarette
releases what's inside of me
as I inhale it into my lungs.
Puff after puff,
I can't seem to get enough.
I blow out everything dying inside of me.
Starring at that cloudy smoke is what I like most.
Slowly reaching its butt,
our time is almost up.
The ashes fall beside me.
Just don't let it remind me.
My lungs feel rough.
I have nothing to puff.
It's now come to an end.
Tomorrow,
we shall meet again.
This cigarette.
For it's just me and this cigarette.

Sparrows' Night

Dust turning to the midnight maddening.
The night of sparrows pulling knots
for the waiting answers.
Coming through over and over.
Letting go,
letting this be,
swaying,
calling to its name.

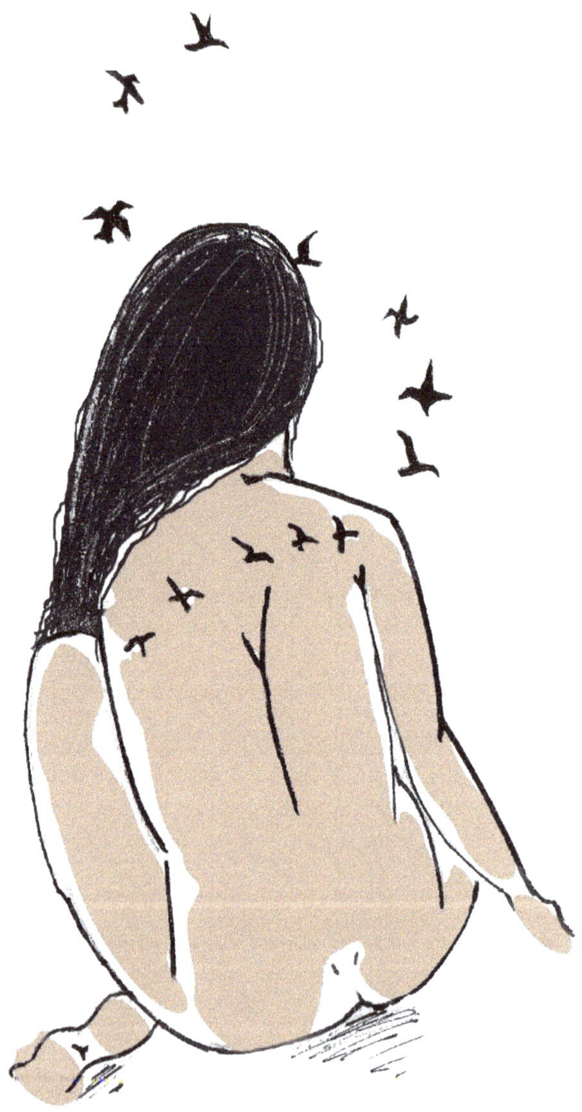

Raven Wings

Beauty in a midnight dance
with letters written on the wings of a raven.
Words of lucid shadows dress us like silk.
See how it moves.
Our raven sends darling showers.
So,
come oh so close.
Its velvet feathers
bring us along this way.
Sleep,
sleep next to me,
but sleepwalk with me
beneath a blue December.

A Day

Just east of the river is where we met.
Have we been here before?
It's a blue day with blue bouquets.
This morning,
this night.
Tell me!
I want to remain.
Blue thunderstorms of pearls grace my face.
I can't hide the blue that is.
Something like a song,
I saw in those eyes.
And I call them blue,
my beautiful blue.

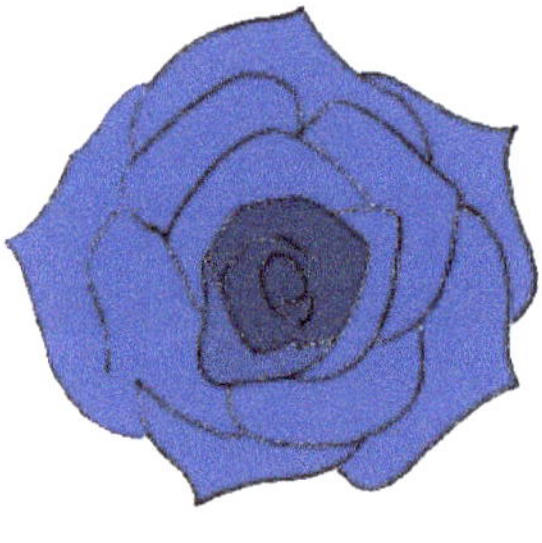

Opal Forever

In a midnight opal hour,
he baptizes me with his shadow graffiti.
A vintage love spilling onto me
the way autumn roses do.
And in my journal,
I wrote about it
and signed it,

Yours forever I am and always.

Whispering Past

Whispers from the past.
The smoke that carries tells a story.
Velvet at the center.
Hit by hit,
keep puffing on it.
Anointed by its purple.
Riddle me this!
I hear a song.
A veiled meaning.
Now here we are.
The wind blows north of the highway,
and I still keep those secrets.

Passionately

Oh,
she loves,
but she doesn't just love.
She loves everything so passionately.
Passionately is how she only sees.

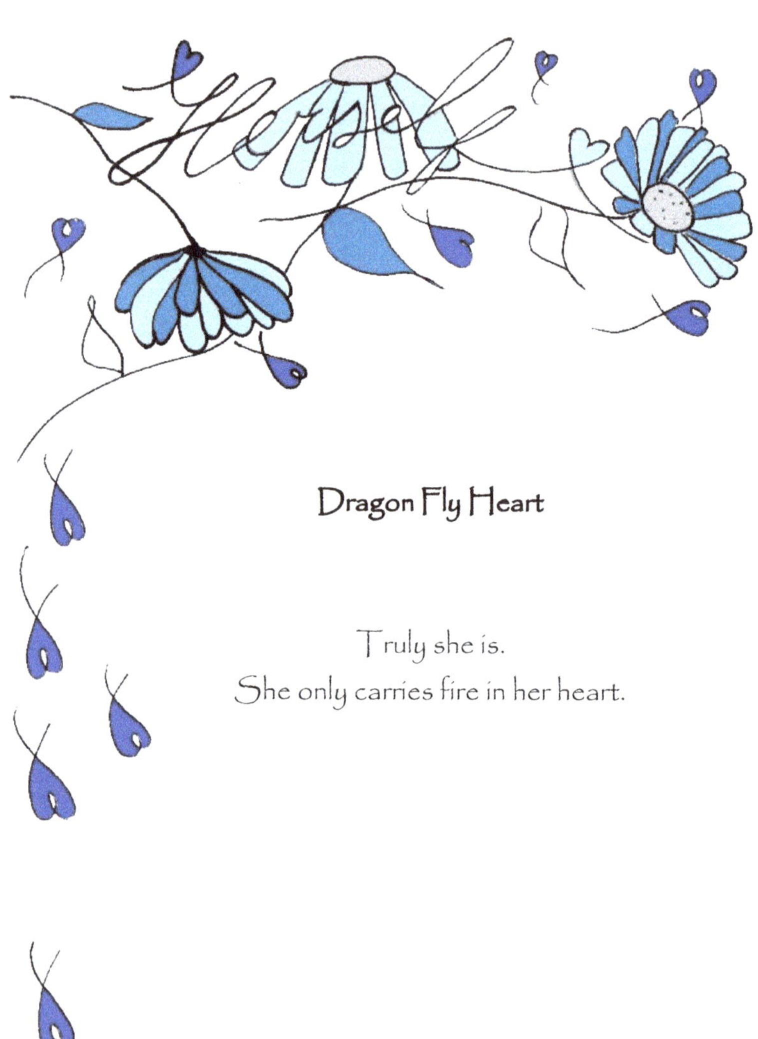

Dragon Fly Heart

Truly she is.
She only carries fire in her heart.

Magic

There is something so beautiful
in the way a woman has been destroyed.

There is magic in her madness.

Him and His Dust

It's about 1 a.m.,
and I'm dressed in satin.
I woke with the feeling of your lips.
Your embers that burn fill in warmth.
There is a sound that I hear
thumping deeply;
it's how your heart beats.
Even before,
I have always felt him.
He and I danced in those same dreams.
We walked amongst the fairies.
His eyes,
the way they light up mine.
His skin,
oh,
his beautiful brown skin.
That same voice that I kept hearing,
it was those images of you,
a side by side view,
a ray of light that kept gleaming through.
The deck that spreads
showed me and you.

And even after,
I felt him even more.
As he arrived,
you,
you came to me covered in fairy dust,
and I lay with him and let it inhale me in.

Cemetery Snowdrops

Breast,
hips,
long hair that blows in his wind.
A shadow wrapped in hungry snowdrops.
Wherever,
whenever it follows.
Cemetery stares against the trees.
Higher and deeper in.
It goes quiet.
Here a shadow awaits.
Taking in the same air that he breathes.
Hoping for just a simple touch.
A shadow that lives for him.
A shadow that wants to exist.

Nocturnal

Teeth only sink in black and white.
It's when everything has been left behind.
What a strange love held for whom shared
the space.
Glimmering shadows,
give yourself away.

24 Hours

It feels a lot colder in here.
Not sure what size bed this is anymore.
24 Hours
Black shades.
Wasted mascara on my face.
No sunlight today.
Finger on his gun
while listening to
"The House of the Rising Sun."
Volume number 9.
24 Hours
At this moment,
I can't be saved.
Tomorrow I'll confess my sins away.
The adrenaline intensifies its level.
24 Hours
His bottle of Remy is now empty.
I've become so numb.
Dark days are on their way.
He's been the ruin of me.
24 Hours

I've been awake for 24 Hours

The Ruby Home

Ruby sunset is the color of your love
through this black heart summer.
We will live to tell a story
of how this came to be.
Watching over,
coming out of the dark
keeps the flame burning.
Say it to me.
Say it with the shades of it.
Smear it with the darkest ruby you hold
before the sunrise calls it home.

Raining Roses

Soaking with the night,
running in a dark ballet,
I stand still under a song
of raining roses.
This will be the place I come to sing.
A place I say goodnight with.
Tell me here if it's to be.
I listen for the echoes while freeing myself.
Raining roses,
still holding on.
Raining roses,
rain down to me.
Picking up the one left for me.

Black Pearls

I drink from the Catholic wine
out in nature in Pagan form.
A veil placed.
Hangs are the five decades
while draped in black pearls.
The highway of heavy waters
drops red roses,
and I write my name in it.
Roam.
I am one with
being of one.
Follow the pearls to its heart shaped place.

Champagne Lips

Each word slips
from a champagne kiss.
Forgotten promises,
that drip from her
ruby red lips.

Dark Mirror

Mirror, mirror,
there are lies on the walls.
Writings of secrets kept in the dark
where skeletons dance along.
Nude by these holes on the floor,
calling to sink in.
I lay on the wood and still talk to the mirror
of dark,
hearing all its songs.
I'll hold the pillow for now,
but
it only wants to see me.

Sea of Whispers

Out here in the desert
left dry,
left me here to die.

My eyes were once brown,
cherry lips turned dirt,
deep fiery pores,
crushed ribs.

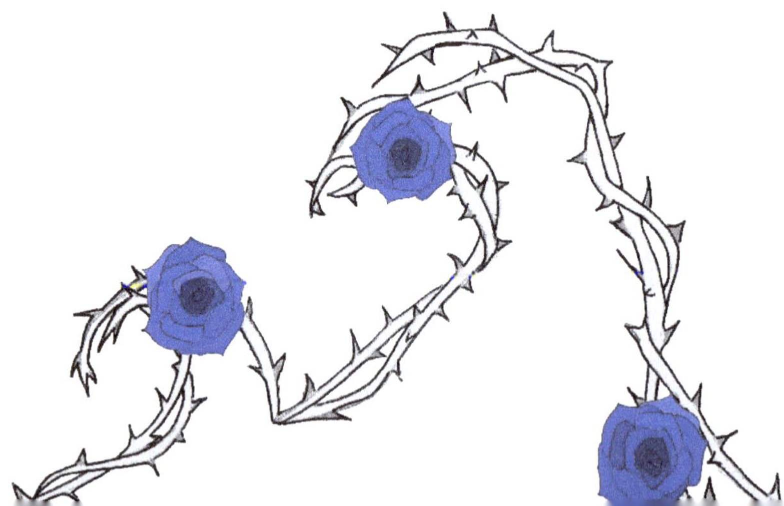

Digging my way through.
Only
I hear the whispers
so far reached
that came from the sea
telling me to come home.

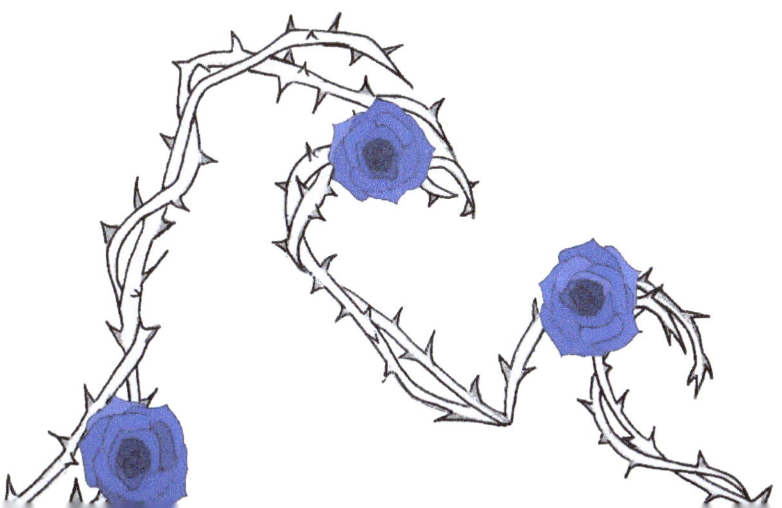

Sea Mystics

Voyages of lost love at the bottom of the sea.
Reefs of letters that never reached.
Pearls float freely.
Precious jewelry in pieces.
Wrecks of paintings.
So many mystics that the mermaids keep.

Thunder

Thunder
hear the sounds.
Vibrations rolling on my lips with grace,
roaring like a wolf heart
and
poetic are her echoes.

Drops

Drops came,
but went.
And after I left,
I didn't bother to look back.
I set fire to the paper that I wrote on
and watched as the ashes spread.
Everything gone,
away it all went.
Flowers in progress to be seen.
I left the past behind
and erased that time.

Daydream in Distance

The fog cleared,
but it's those drops of ice crystals
that sometimes creep near.
A passageway filled with low clouds.
Only seeing you half way.
Uncertainties,
faded memories.
A language no longer spoken.
As it gets drearier,
the mist of a daydream washes aside.

Seven

Seven.
I count the days.
Hoping the nights become shorter.

Eight.
On the same night,
I hope it to be the last.
I come to my knees.
I talk in an alto clinching on to something.
Let it go,
I guess.

Nine.
Keep holding to it.
Maybe?
I'll leave this here.

Ten.
It's too heavy now.
Maybe I'll see what it will be?
Oneness.

Eleven.
Another day here.
Maybe tonight will be it?

This has always been deeper than anyone,
deeper than anything.
Moving with the flames on
twelve.

It's always been you.
Even when I didn't know,
it was always you.

Thirteen.
Covered in.
Fourteen.

I count in sevens.

That Upstairs Apartment

It was in that apartment where I felt most alone.
It was my home,
but still alone.
I could hear the rain hit the window,
the ice in the freezer as it fell.
I could hear the AC kick on,
the June Bugs as they hit the side screen.

Mostly,
because I sat there in silence
listening to my thoughts:
wondering,
thinking,
trying really.
I couldn't exactly move from that same spot,
couldn't even talk.

Only,
felt the silence,
sat in silence,
my silence.

As I was soaking,
I was also hoping.
But those things kept forming.

It was in that apartment,
that upstairs apartment,
where I felt most alone.
It was also in that apartment
where I began
to transform.

Stained Rose

Four drops onto
what was once a white rose.
Stained of hidden things
and through the ice
of dances in the dark.

A Nightingale

Nightingale,
as words sang,
it places a stain
as if it were only for me.
I am here to sleep.
Acoustic becomes me.
Sweetest dreams
are the whispers.
It helps lay down the demons to
sleep better with me.

Cemetery Secrets

I followed him
inside these gates he calls home.
Worn out leather jacket,
smell of rusted cologne.
The way he plays his guitar...
e l e c t r i c i t y.
I fell in love with his ghost.
Meetings before each dawn,
black roses wait for me,
but if only he could speak.
Orgasms from each string
fire through me.
These moments.
We keep secrets in his cemetery.

Valley of Love

In the valley,
the same place I come to pray,
here
in the field of lilies is where I found my love.
And my dear,
I could not see myself without.
We dipped our bodies in a perfume bath
that waited for me.
A song
from love making that makes red wine.

Liberated

The gates.
They now extract as gold.
Once as new.
Speak to me.
I heard the bells ring.
As I walked through,
the shackles broke loose.
Have you ever smelled the snow?
White flakes hit my nose,
falling onto me like milk and honey.
This is the great promise.
I feel my certainty.

What an angelic scene.
Let the foot prints create their hints.
Opening of eyes,
hands held,
kisses to each.
So far,
I have arisen from.
Yet, so much more.
As I hummed,
as I did before while "the caged bird" did sing.
At last!

Blue Soul

Scattered pages on the floor
from the letters I want to send.
I feel the mood of your soul
as I walk through the door.
I hear the blue sparrow from the windowsill
that follows me around
and I start to sing its song.
I paint all those dreams in wood smoke.
And I wear something blue in remembrance of
you.
6 letters grace the sky.
I sit in the driveway while seated in your color
blue.
Here is still only half of us:
a place to run to,
a place I run with,
a place to find you.
Your soul.
That blue soul.

Reborn

I hate it when I can't seem to sleep.
Up at 2 am.
Thinking,
drowning in carnations.
It's raining here.
Deep breaths,
just deep breaths.
Oil and water.
Unplug.
Maybe now is the time to be reborn?

War of my Roses

Scattered,
it became distorted,
estranged.
Love me,
love me not.
Here's my offering,
a red bouquet.
It's the month of December.
Forgive me as I let it fall.
I felt the concrete floor.
I might have lost the will for this.
Faded to grey,
but not quite to black,
not at least
the darkness.
I don't want to be in love with it.
Here I am,
holding the words in my hands,
opened to say 23.
Oh,
Queen I summon thee.
Awaken me.

And suddenly,
lightning raids the brown skin
that I am covered in.
Restoration.
Behold this paradise I see,
the ascension of Me,
raised at the highest.
Crown Me as I fall in love with Me.
Once again,
it falls so beautifully.

My rose ink drops
mark every spot.

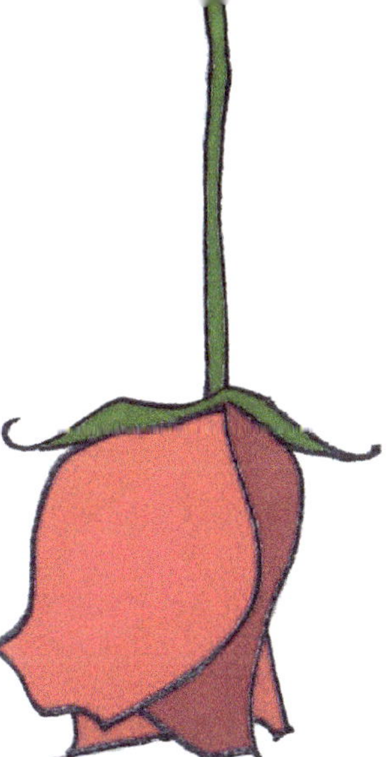

Acknowledgements

I would like to thank those involved in the process of creating my first poetry book.

A big thank you to my editor, Ashley Jane, for her patience and with the help of putting this all together. It flows so beautifully! To my good friend, Sandra Solis, for creating the illustrations for the cover and interior.

And thank you to everyone for taking the time to read Blue Roses. Your support means a lot.

About the Author

Y. Zambrano is a writer born and raised in Houston, Texas. She received her B.S. in Psychology from the University of Houston Downtown. She began writing poetry in 2013 as a therapeutic approach which has led her to creating her own art in word form.

www.ingramcontent.com/pod-product-compliance
Ingram Content Group UK Ltd.
Pitfield, Milton Keynes, MK11 3LW, UK
UKHW062306290726
14090UKWH00018B/903

9 780578 750521